Rebel's
BIBLE

By David Wilkerson

Rebel's BIBLE

DAVID WILKERSON

Fleming H. Revell Company
Old Tappan, New Jersey

Scripture quotations are from the *King James Version of the Bible.*

SBN 8007-0411-8

TO
my mother

Contents

Introduction

Che Guevara said,

"In fact, the eruption of the Latin American struggle has begun.

Will its storm center be

In Venezuela, Guatemala, Colombia,

Peru, Ecuador?

Are today's skirmishes only manifestations of a restlessness

That has not come to fruition?

The outcome of today's struggles does not matter. . . .

What is definite is the decision to struggle

Which matures every day,

The consciousness of the need for revolutionary change,

And the certainty that it is possible."

Che is dead,

But he is now being interpreted

By thousands of young rebels around the world.

The source of a rebel's inspiration

Is the most important thing to revolution.

Spurious sources create spurious solutions.

Rebels will discredit themselves

And lose all equilibrium

Unless a new, sound, ideological foundation is found.

The Bible is that foundation.
It is a strategy for taking power.
No glorious mission can be fulfilled without it.
Marxism has been exhausted.
It no longer functions in man's newest struggles.
Rebel's Bible is a call to mobilization
And to a spiritual struggle
Founded on truth revealed by God's Word.
Let every rebel and guerilla understand
God speaks to every problem of this generation
And it is not propaganda.
Fractionalism has undermined all revolutions,
But God's Word transcends all revolutionary strata
To unite men in one class—
The redeemed class.
The last revolution has begun—
A spiritual one—
Not one of insurrection
But resurrection.
It is a revolution with an inate antibody
That will counteract all rebel vanguards.
Once and for all the ownership of revolution
Will be eternally established
And God will still be sitting
King of the flood.

DAVID WILKERSON

Rebel's
BIBLE

DRESS ME, JESUS

Put on the whole armour of God, that ye may be able to stand against the wiles of the devil (Ephesians 6:11).

Dear Jesus,
You told me to *resist the devil* and he would flee
    from me,
But I have no resistance.
You have all the power and resistance I'll ever need,
So give me power to resist.
You told me I could move my mountains
If I had faith even as a mustard seed;
Yet my mountain won't move
Even though my faith in you is as great
As I can conceive it.
You made the heavens and earth:
Please move my mountain.
You said, "Flee the very appearance of evil!"
So I ran hard,
But sin overtook me
In my finest hour of effort.

You have power
Over all the power of the enemy
With miracles, signs and wonders.
Deliver me from the trap of Satan.
I don't even have the strength to put on the whole
    armor,
So dress me as my armor-bearer.
Do for me what I know I cannot do for myself.

HOW TO BECOME A JEW, A CHRISTIAN OR A COMMUNIST

But he is a Jew, which is one inwardly; and circumcision is that of the heart, in the spirit, and not in the letter; whose praise is not of men, but of God (Romans 2:29).

Not every man born a Jew is one.
He is not a Jew who is one only outwardly.
He is not a Jew who denies the spirit,
The tradition, the calling, of a Jew;
Yet *he is a Jew who is one inwardly*

By faith becoming so in the heart.
This is the way of all life.
A Christian is one who receives the spirit of Christ,
By faith becoming so in the heart.
A Communist need not carry a card
To be one.
He can deny to the world he is a Communist,
Yet if inwardly he embraces the spirit,
The tradition, the calling, of a Communist—
He is one inwardly.
What a man is cannot be determined
By the words and praises of men,
But by what God sees in the heart.
As a man *thinketh in his heart,*
So is he!

I AM YOUR GOD

Fear thou not; for I am with thee: be not dismayed; for I am thy God: I will strengthen thee; yea, I will help thee; yea, I will uphold thee with the right hand of my righteousness (Isaiah 41:10).

The God of Abraham, Isaac and Jacob
Is your God
To deliver and strengthen you
As He did your fathers—
To help you,
Uphold you,
Keep you,
Fear not: be not dismayed.
They who know Him as their God
Shall do exploits
And become strong.
He will still your enemies and avengers.
He will make His strength perfect
In your weakness,
For in His hand is all power and might
To do for you exceedingly above all
You could ask or think.
To you he speaks,

"I am with you,
I am your God,
I will help,
You."

A CHOCOLATE-COATED,
NOUGAT-CENTERED GOD!

And all things, whatsoever ye shall ask in prayer, believing, ye shall receive (*Matthew 21:22*).

Does God really answer prayer
If I simply believe
And ask?
Will my harvest flourish,
My sickness vanish,
Temptations dissolve into nothingness?
Will He protect my travels,
Keeping me from accidents and harm?
And what about all the chocolate-coated, nougat-
    centered things

I keep longing for,
Like wealth, prosperity and promotion?
There is a catch!
God promises to give only that asked for in prayer.
Prayer is closeness to God.
It is selfless communion,
Holy worship and praise.
A man who is in prayer
Does not ask selfishly:
He knows God answers people, not prayer.
And people in prayer
Ask according to God's will,
Because they understand it.

I AM WEAK

*Have mercy upon me, O Lord; for I am
weak: O Lord, heal me; for my bones are
vexed (Psalms 6:2).*

Don't get mad at me, God,
Or in anger whip me.
My soul is confused.

How long will it be so?
All night long
I make my bed to swim in tears.
I am weary of groaning:
Grief consumes me.
My soul is being torn to pieces—
Let my wickedness come to an end.
Mischief has been conceived in me and
I have brought forth falsehood.
I dug a pit
And fell in.
My dealings have come down
Upon my own head.
Have mercy upon me
For I am weak.
O Lord,
Heal me:
My bones ache.
Hear the voice of my weeping
And wipe away
My tears.

HISTORY IS NO LESSON

. . . no man knoweth either love or hatred by all that is before them (Ecclesiastes 9:1).

Man cannot learn from history
For we are but of yesterday.
Our days on earth are but a shadow.
Generation rises after generation:
All things happen alike to all.
There is one event to the righteous
And to the wicked,
To the good and to the clean
And to the unclean.
History has failed
To teach man any lessons
On love and hate.
He refuses to listen,
Stopping the ears so he cannot hear
Lest he should understand
And be converted.
Our fathers loved and hated
And are dead in their trespasses,
But to him that is joined to the living
There is hope;
For a living dog is better than a dead lion.

We too shall be history.
Our love, hatred and envy will die
And our memory shall be forgotten,
Leaving history without a lesson.

HEZEKIAH—THE MAN WHO BEAT A DEATH RAP!

*In those days was Hezekiah sick unto death.
And Isaiah the prophet the son of Amoz came
unto him, and said unto him, Thus saith the
Lord, Set thine house in order for thou shalt
die, and not live (Isaiah 38:1).*

He was a King riding the crest of victory,
Delivered miraculously by God
From King Sennacherib's army.
He was wealthy and renowned
When sickness struck,
Bringing him to the brink of death.
The prophet warned,

"Get ready to die
It's all over for you."
But the king loved life,
And turning his face to the wall
Cried, and prayed to the Lord
For a new lease on life.
God heard and gave him fifteen more years.
But how should a man live
Who has won over death?
As so many do who survive
A close call with death.
Should he not live each day gratefully,
Giving himself humbly to God and mankind?
But the way of human flesh is not so.
The king began to glory in his own worth—
He sank in the mud of materialism,
Parading his treasures before foreigners.
A second message by the prophet was sounded
Of judgment on his posterity
For pride and ingratitude.
And how many today have been given a new lease
On life,
Only to spend their borrowed years
In selfish pursuit of things
Which have no value?
Eternity will reveal

It would have been better
For some to die
Rather than beat the rap.

PEOPLE ARE GRASS

The grass withereth, the flower fadeth: because the spirit of the Lord bloweth upon it: surely the people is grass (Isaiah 40:7).

The grass withers and the flowers fade
When the sun and rain are withdrawn.
People are like grass
And the flowers that bloom
Bright and fresh with the dew of life.
And when man is green and in full bloom
He thinks he shall live forever
Full of fragrance, vitality and youth.
But all life is sustained
By the spirit of the Lord,
Which from the beginning
Has been breathed into man.

So let all men understand
Life is but a vapor,
A fragile green blade,
A short lived blossom
That will fade and wither.
And God will gather everything that dies
Either to be burned in heaps
Or to be resurrected to new life.
Except a seed die
It cannot bring forth fruit.

RUSSIA AND THE UNITED STATES— TWO LITTLE DROPS IN A BUCKET!

Behold, the nations are as a drop of a bucket, and are counted as the small dust of the balance: behold, he taketh up the isles as a very little thing (Isaiah 40:15).

All *nations are as a drop of a bucket*
In God's sight,
Including the United States and Russia—

The leading powers.
The isles of the sea,
Japan, England, Austrialia,
Are small drops in the same bucket—
Considered as little things
In God's sight.
Let them all glory in their armies,
Their space exploits and their wealth.
They are as dust
Measured on God's scale.
All nations before Him are as nothing:
They are counted to Him less than nothing.
He sits *upon the circle of the earth*
And nations *are as grasshoppers,*
Yet He gave His only Son to die
For mankind
Because He is willing for no one to perish,
But have everlasting life.

GOD HASN'T EVEN FAINTED

Hast thou not known? hast thou not heard, that
the everlasting God, the Lord, the Creator of
the ends of the earth, fainteth not, neither is
weary? there is no searching of his under-
standing (Isaiah 40:28).

There is an ignorance of God
That supposes He no longer reveals Himself
To mankind in his crises and needs—
That He is either dead or asleep,
Unable to monitor or guide the steps of man.
But who is man to measure God?
To whom will we liken Him
Or compare Him?
Hast thou not known?
Hast thou not heard?
The everlasting Creator,
The God of the ends of the world,
Neither slumbers nor sleeps.
He *fainteth not,*
Neither is weary,
But they that trust in Him
Shall renew their faith and *strength.*

They shall fly as eagles:
They shall run and not be weary,
Nor shall they faint.

ANYBODY REMEMBER KHRUSHCHEV?

*Thou shalt seek them, and shalt not find
them, even them that contended with thee:
they that war against thee shall be as nothing,
and as a thing of nought (Isaiah 41:12).*

Khrushchev, the Russian strongman,
Thumped his shoe at the United Nations
And cried, "We will bury you!"
Anyone remember him?
Or Hitler?
Mussolini or Hirohito?
Thou shalt seek them
And not find them.
They all made war,
Holding the earth in fear,
Causing the masses to tremble.

Their names were etched in terror,
But now they are nothing—
Gone forever.
Each new day spawns a new breed
Of despots, dictators and devils,
But tomorrow they will vanish,
Trampled like grasshoppers,
When their cup of iniquity is filled.
Never to be forgotten
Are men of PEACE.

THE HORROR OF HOROSCOPES

Thou art wearied in the multitude of thy counsels. Let now the astrologers, the star-gazers, the monthly prognosticators, stand up, and save thee from these things that shall come upon thee (Isaiah 47:13).

Beware of astrologers,
Star gazers and monthly prognosticators
Who try to predict

Things that shall come upon you.
They offer a multitude of counsels
On how to avoid mischief and danger,
Yet with all their advice
Not one of them can save a single person
From the things that are coming.
These prognosticators
That now weary our land
Are proud and lifted up,
Trusting in foolish enchantments
And sorceries.
Their wisdom and knowledge is perverted.
And often so foolish
Not even Satan or demons
Wish to be blamed.
If their prophecies be truth,
Let them stand up and save somebody
From the evil they foresee.

THE FURNACE OF AFFLICTION

> *. . . I have chosen thee in the furnace of affliction (Isaiah 48:10).*

There is a furnace of affliction
For God's chosen to endure.
White ashes are eaten like bread
As the Father chastens those he loves.
Now no chastening for the present seems joyous,
But grievous and bitter;
Yet *afterward it yieldeth*
The peaceable fruit of righteousness.
The furnace is but for a moment—
To walk in is eternal glory.
Before the furnace experience
Man went astray,
But the fury of fiery affliction
Leads men to keep God's Word.
Despise not the chastening of the Lord
Nor the furnace of affliction,
For whom the Lord loveth
He correcteth,
And He promises
To bring the afflicted one forth
As pure gold
TRIED IN THE FIRE.

THE DEVIL'S CHILDREN

*In this the children of God are manifest, and
the children of the devil: whosoever doeth not
righteousness is not of God, neither he that
loveth not his brother (I John 3:10).*

The devil's children
Are clearly defined by God
As those who refuse to do righteousness
And those who love not their brother.
God's message *from the beginning* [of time is]
That we should love one another.
*We know that we have passed from death unto
    life*
When we learn to love our brother.
He that loveth not his brother
Still abides *in death.*
Whoso *hateth his brother is a murderer,*
And no murderer shall enter eternal life.
Whoso hath this world's good,
And seeth his brother have need,
*And shutteth up his bowels of compassion from
    him—*
How can he say that the love of God dwells in
    him?
Let us not love in word [or] *tongue,*

But in deed and in truth.
He that loveth not his brother
Is a child of the devil
And beyond hope.

GOD IS INTEGRATED

If a man say, I love God, and hateth his
brother, he is a liar: for he that loveth not his
brother who he hath seen, how can he love
God whom he hath not seen? And this com-
mandment have we from him, That he that
loveth God love his brother also (I John
4:20-21).

Never believe what a man says about love,
If he segregates himself from a brother
Of any color or race,
For there is no fear in love
Perfect love casteth out all *fear*
Because fear hath torment.
How can one say he loves God

And believes in equality,
While at the same time he is tormented
By the fear of a brother
He mistrusts or dislikes?
If a man cannot love his brother
Whom he can see,
How can he love God
Who is unseen?
God has commanded men everywhere
To love his brother
As God has loved him—
For God is love.

REBEL RABBLE

These are murmurers, complainers, walking after their own lusts; and their mouth speaketh great swelling words, having men's persons in admiration because of advantage (Jude 16).

There are rebels who have something to say.
Others spew out rabble,
Murmuring and complaining,
Wallowing in their own lusts—
Like clouds without water
Carried about with the wind,
Trees with withered fruit,
Raging waves of the sea
Foaming out their own shame—
Wandering stars.
Their *mouth speaketh great swelling words*
Claiming to be free to speak only truth.
There is method to their madness.
Every word is spoken in a design
To gain an advantage
With every other rebel of their kind,
For they seek to be admired
And praised

By their own establishment.
Capitalism is not nearly as competitive
As revolution.

BELIEVE IT OR NOT

 . . . *whatsoever is not of faith is sin* (*Romans 14:23*).

Believe it or not,
That is the question.
Did Jesus really walk on water,
Heal lepers,
Raise the dead,
Make the blind to see,
Cause the winds and waves to obey,
Cast out devils,
Heal lunatics,
And turn water into wine?
To believe all of that
A man would have to believe in miracles!
Yet a man cannot believe in Christ at all,

Unless he believes in miracles—
His resurrection
And ascension.
He is either dead or alive,
And if alive—
It is a miracle!
And all He ever did was miraculous.
Believe it all;
That is faith!

NOW I LAY ME DOWN TO SLEEP

*I laid me down and slept; I awaked; for the
Lord sustained me (Psalms 3:5).*

God,
How I want to sleep!
They are *increased that trouble me.*
Many are they that rise up against me.
They say
There is no help for him in God.
Tens of thousands of people

Are arrayed against me.
O Lord,
Are you still a shield?
Can you lift up my head?
I will cry to the Lord
To hear me from His Holy hill.
If He will sustain me,
I will lay me down
And sleep.
I will awake
And He shall make my enemy
My footstool.

ATTACKING THE HEART

Keep thy heart with all diligence; for out of it are the issues of life (*Proverbs 4:23*).

Watch your heart,
The one encased in your soul.
For as a man *thinketh in his* own *heart,*
So is he.

Out of the abundance of the heart,
The mouth speaks
And all things that proceed out of the mouth,
Come forth from the heart,
And they defile the man.
A good man stores up treasure in his heart
So he can bring forth that which is good.
An evil man
Bringeth forth evil from an evil treasure.
It is with the heart
That man believes.
He can confess faith
Only when it overflows from the heart,
For out of the heart
Are all the issues of life.
Those are on good ground,
Which from an honest and good heart
Hear the truth
And keep it,
Bringing forth fruit
With patience.

WHO AM I?

*Though I were perfect, yet would I not know
my soul: I would despise my life (Job 9:21).*

God seems so great and big;
I seem so small and imperfect.
He commands the sun and it rises;
I break to pieces in a tempest.
He spreads out the heavens and walks on waves,
But He goes by me and I see Him not.
He rules the chamber of stars.
If I call to Him in the heavens
And He answered,
Yet I would not believe He heard my voice.
I feel like God has wounded me
Without cause.
He is the Judge,
But who will plead for me?
When I try to justify myself,
My own mouth condemns me.
The feeling grows
That even if I were perfect,
I would not know myself.
I would still despise life
Because

We are really of yesterday
And know nothing,
For life is a shadow.

ESCAPE

Deliver me in thy righteousness, and cause me to escape: incline thine ear unto me, and save me (Psalms 71:2).

Confusion!
Ever since I was young,
I am as a wonder unto many.
My adversaries say
God has forsaken him—
Sore and great troubles are on every side.
Deliver me, God,
Cause me to escape.
Turn Your ear my way.
Save me.
Forsake me not.
Deliver the needy when they cry,

The poor, also,
And him that hath no helper.
Redeem mankind's soul
From deceit and violence.
Come down like rain
On new mown grass
With an abundance of peace.
We will put our trust in You,
But let us not be put to confusion.
Send out a commandment
To save us.
Be our fortress—
Our way of escape.

SOMEBODY UNDERSTANDS

O Lord, thou hast searched me, and known me (Psalms 139:1).

Nobody understands me
But God.
He understands my deep thoughts.

There is not a word in my tongue,
But God knows it altogether.
He has me hemmed in;
His hand is laid upon me.
Such knowledge is so high,
I cannot attain unto it.
There are times
Darkness surrounds me,
Yet He searches my heart
And knows it.
He sees the wicked ways in me.
Only His wisdom
Can figure me out.
In the day when I cry to Him,
He answers,
And strengthenest me with strength
In my soul.
Darkness and light are both alike to Him.
He understands my darkness
And will give me light.
He understands me.

THE SECRET OF STRENGTH

The righteous also shall hold on his way, and he that hath clean hands shall be stronger and stronger (Job 17:9).

Men are losing their grip on life:
Mockers abound—
Provocation on all sides.
Wise men can't be found.
When beds are made in darkness
Corruption has become their father.
It is time
For the innocent to be astonished by this
And *stir up himself against the hypocrite.*
O that one might plead for a man with God,
So the righteous may hold onto their way
And the light of the wicked put out—
The spark of his fire die.
The way of the wicked is slippery
And sin is a reproach,
Devouring strength;
But *he that hath clean hands*
Shall be stronger
And stronger.

THE ROOT OF FEAR

*If iniquity be in thine hand, put it far away,
and let not wickedness dwell in thy tabernac-
les. For then shalt thou lift up thy face without spot; yea, thou shalt be stedfast, and shalt
not fear (Job 11:14, 15).*

All fear can be traced
To a spot
Of sin and secret iniquity
Harbored in a man's heart.
He has the power in his hand
To put it away.
Despising the riches of God's grace,
His . . . forbearance and long suffering,
He continues in his evil way,
Allowing in his own life
What he condemns in others,
Becoming a law unto himself.
He seeks to be God's favored exception
To escape wrath and tribulation.
But God is no respecter of persons,
Judging all alike,
Promising glory, honor and peace
To those who put evil away.

And then he shall lift up his face without spot.
He shall be steadfast
And shall not fear,
For only where sin lies at the door
Is man afraid.

WHO CAN MAKE DIRT CLEAN?

*Who can bring a clean thing out of an un-
clean? not one* (*Job 14:4*).

Man that is born of a woman
Lives so little,
So *full of trouble*—
Cut down like a flower in bloom—
Vanishing like a shadow.
The boundaries of his life have been assigned,
His employment by the Almighty sealed,
Every step numbered,
Until his appointed death.
The very thought seems dirty,
Depraved.

So man lays down,
Hoping some day to raise up again
When the wrath has passed
To a clean, new world
Without pain and mourning.
Yet man's every *transgression*
Is sealed up in a bag
And God watches over his sin.
Who can make dirt clean?
Who can turn death to victory?
Not one
Human,
Only God!

HATE

Hatred stirreth up strifes: but love covereth all sins (Proverbs 10:12).

Whosoever hateth his brother is a murderer
And is full of madness.
Hatred is the fruit of wickedness

And he that maketh a sport of it
Only stirreth up strife.
Love covers and forgives all,
But hatred is the language of violence.
He that hideth hatred
With lying lips . . .
Is a fool;
In his mouth are a multitude of words
Of little worth.
As a whirlwind that passeth
And is no more,
So is the wicked who hate.
As vinegar to the teeth
And smoke to the eyes,
So is the hater.
To them that inhabit the earth,
The prating fool
Shall fall.

THE LANGUAGE OF REVOLUTION

There is that speaketh like the piercing of a sword: but the tongue of the wise is health (Proverbs 12:18).

With great and swelling words
The revolutionaries speak.
Like the piercing of a sword,
They lash with their tongues
The established order of the day.
An evil man diggeth up evil
And in his lips there is a burning fire,
The unquenchable fire of hell.
But *the wicked* man shall be *snared*
By the transgression of his own *lips.*
He that keepeth his mouth,
Keepeth his life,
But he that openeth wide his mouth
Shall have destruction.
For righteous men hate lying lips
And lips that have no healing.
The lamp of the wicked shall be put out
And his lips sealed;
For wicked language

Shall be overthrown
And the tongue of the wise
Shall send forth health.

FREE AMONG THE DEAD!

Free among the dead, like the slain that lie in the grave, whom thou rememberest no more: and they are cut off from thy hand (Psalms 88:5).

O Lord God,
I have cried to you
Night and day,
For my soul is full of troubles.
I am at the bottom of the pit.
I am weak,
Having no strength.
Free among the dead,
I feel cut off from you.
In darkness—
Suffering your wrath,

Afflicted by waves of agony,
Even friends don't understand me.
Why do you cast me off?
Why do you hide your face?
What good is freedom
If I must walk among the dead?
Shall the dead arise and praise thee?
But the Lord God is strong.
He is faithful.
I will sing of his mercies and compassion.
He will raise the dead
And we shall all be free.

NO NAME IN THE STREET!

His remembrance shall perish from the earth, and he shall have no name in the street (Job 18:17).

Black and white,
Rich and poor,
They have dried up by the roots.

Every branch cut off,
Scattered like brimstone
Over the earth's skin.
Cast down by their own counsel,
Tearing themselves apart with their own anger,
Marked like beasts,
Reputed vile by the tabernacle people,
Like a candle dying—
Drawn into a net by their own feet,
Terrors shall make them *afraid on every side.*
Hunger bitten,
Confidence uprooted—
Chased out of this world.
And those who came after
Will be astonished by this day,
That so many
Knew not God
And were removed
With no name left in the street.

ARMY DAY

Come near, ye nations, to hear; and harken, ye people let the earth hear, and all that is therein; the world, and all things that come forth of it. For the indignation of the Lord is upon all nations, and his fury upon all their armies: he hath delivered them to the slaughter (Isaiah 34:1-2).

Let all *the earth hear*
For God has bathed His sword in blood.
It shall come down as a curse
With indignation and wrath
Upon the armies of all nations.
They are appointed to slaughter;
Their slain shall fall as leaves.
The *stink shall come up* from *their carcasses*
And the mountains will flow *with their blood.*
The lands soaked with it.
For it is a day of vengeance
And God shall roll back the heavens
As a scroll.
Streams will turn into pitch
And dust into brimstone.
The land shall burn with fervent heat,

For nations that live by the sword
Shall die
By His sword,
When God pours His wrath upon the armies of
the world.

ALWAYS PREGNANT— BUT NEVER A PARENT!

. . . this day is a day of trouble, and of rebuke, and of blasphemy: for the children are come to the birth, and there is not strength to bring forth (Isaiah 37:3).

Society is always pregnant
But never a parent.
Ideas and programs are formed
In the wombs of brilliant minds;
The announcements are made
And all men wait
For the promise to spring forth alive.
But when the appointed time arrives

And the child comes to the moment of birth,
There is no strength to deliver—
Not even a miscarriage—
The child dies in the womb.
It is a day of rebuke and blasphemy.
There is a grave somewhere on this earth
Where these dead brain children
Are buried and forgotten.
And there is no time to mourn,
For already Mother Society is again pregnant
With another promise
That will never be born,
Because there is no moral strength
To deliver.

SIN KILLS ME!

For sin, taking occasion by the command-ment, deceived me, and by it slew me (Romans 7:11).

Every new day is a revelation
Of how sinful my heart is.
I claim to be dead to the world
And he that is dead is freed from sin.
The Scripture warns me,
Let not sin therefore reign in your mortal body—
Don't yield to unrighteousness,
Resist the devil,
Let no sin have dominion over you.
Walk in holiness
With clean hands and pure heart.
Walk in His Spirit
And you will not fulfill the lusts of the flesh.
This is all truth
And it makes me miserable
For I am weak.
The sin in me mocks these commandments
And it kills me.
Oh! wretched man that I am!
Wanting to be perfect and holy,

I am sinful and hell bent.
Who can deliver me
From this horrible dilemma?
Only Christ!
And then only by faith
That he will give me a new resurrection
Out of my hell into His grace.

THE WAY OUT

*Thy way is in the sea, and thy path in the
great waters, and thy footsteps are not known
(Psalms 77:19).*

God has promised
To make a way of escape
From temptation—
A way that leads to the sea,
A path into deep waters.
*I complained
And my spirit was overwhelmed.*
A way of escape?

Into the sea?
Deep and great waters?
I communed with my heart
And made diligent search.
The deep waters surround me;
I swim in a sea of trial.
Has the Lord cast me off?
Does He no longer favor me?
Is His mercy gone forever?
Hath God forgotten to be gracious?
In anger has He shut me up
In a sea of confusion?
Then I remembered,
Thou leadest Thy people like a flock
By the hand of Moses
Into great waters.
The waters saw thee, O God
And *they were afraid.*
The depths . . . were troubled;
They obeyed
And the waters parted.
I too will walk by faith
Into great waters,
And if I cannot hear Your footsteps behind me,
I will walk on.
I will remember

How *He divided the sea*
And . . . made the waters to stand as an heap.
I will pass through
With them.

DEEP WATER

I sink in deep mire, where there is no stand-
ing: I am come into deep waters, where the
floods overflow me (Psalms 69:2).

Save me, O God,
For my soul is being flooded
With foolishness.
My sins are not hidden from Thee.
I am sinking
With no place to stand;
I am in deep water.
Floods overflow me;
I wait for God to rescue me.
My throat is dry
From calling on Him.

I weep and chasten my soul,
Mocking my own weakness.
Hear me speedily, God,
And don't hide your face.
I need a comforter:
Turn to me with tender mercy.
Deliver me out of this mire.
Let me not sink.
Save me from this deep water:
I am in real trouble—
Danger.
Don't *let the deep swallow me up.*
Let not the pit shut her mouth upon me.
Make haste, O God,
Tarry not;
You are my help
And deliverer.

POWER OVER FEAR

What time I am afraid, I will trust in thee
(Psalms 56:3).

I am afraid.
Fearfulness and trembling are come upon me;
Terrors of death are fallen upon me.

AFRAID

Because there is more evil in me than good,
Lying rather than righteousness,
Weakness instead of strength.
I am like an unripe olive tree
Without fruit.
Oh, that I had wings like a dove,
I would fly away
And be at rest.
I would hasten my escape
From the windy storm
And tempest.

AFRAID

God may cast me off
And curse this green tree,
For He came seeking fruit
And found none.

AFRAID

So I can but trust in Him.
I will call
And He will save me.
He shall hear my voice
And deliver my soul in peace
From the *battle*
That is *against me.*
He will bottle my tears.
God is for me.
He will keep my feet from falling,
That I may walk before Him
IN THE LIGHT OF THE LIVING

AWAKE—GOD!

*Awake, why sleepest thou, O Lord? arise, cast
us not off for ever (Psalms 44:23).*

God,
Why do you seem to hide Your face
And forget my affliction—
My battle?

I am *bowed down to the dust.*
My belly clings to the earth;
I feel cast off—
Put to shame—
Unworthy.
You seem to have given me over
Like meat for wolves.
My confusion is continually on my mind
And still I have not forgotten Thee;
My *heart is not turned back.*
In the very shadow of death,
I have stretched out my hand
To a God
Who knoweth all secrets.
Like a sheep
Going to slaughter
I am condemned.
Awake!
Why sleepest Thou,
O Lord?
Anoint me *with the oil of gladness,*
Rejoice my soul,
Be present in my trouble,
Break the cords of my sin.
Restore me,
Comfort me,

Assure me
That your ear is open to my cry—
That you have heard
And all things are working together
For good.

THE BOTTOMLESS PIT

*Deep calleth unto deep at the noise of thy
waterspouts: all thy waves and thy billows are
gone over me (Psalms 42:7).*

There is a bottomless pit
Inside me—
A chasm so deep,
So wide,
It is a whirlpool
Of affliction.
My soul is so thirsty for God,
Tears have been my meat night and day.
I pour out my soul in me.
Why am I so cast down?

Why do I mourn?
Waves and billows swallow me up.
My soul is despondent
And I cannot tell you why.
Why cannot I appear before God
And tell Him of my complaint?
Of the endless loneliness,
The fightings within,
Yearnings
Of the Niagara
Crashing through my soul.
The whole world cries,
"Where is God
When the enemy comes in
Like a flood?"
Hope in Him,
In His promise
That floods shall not overflow thee
Nor swallow thee up.
He sits King of the flood.
Let the ungodly say in his heart
God hath forgotten,
But let saints in deep waters
Turn with hope and song
To the Rock,
The Shelter,
In time of storm.

STRANGE WOMEN

*And why wilt thou, my son, be ravished with
a strange woman, and embrace the bosom of a
stranger?* (*Proverbs* 5:20).

"*The lips of a strange woman*
Drop as an honey comb, and
Her mouth is smoother than oil:
But her end is bitter
As wormwood . . .
A twoedged sword.
Her feet go down to death. . . .
Remove thy way far from her,
And come not nigh . . . her house. . . .
Drink waters out of thine own cistern,
And running waters
Out of thine own well.
Let your fountain be blessed . . .
With the wife of thy youth.
Be . . . ravished with her . . ."
At all times.
"*Why . . . be ravished with* another *woman*
And embrace the bosom
Of a stranger?"
For God sees all.
Man's infidelity shall enslave the wicked

And he shall be held
By *the cords of his* own *sins*.
He shall die without heeding *instructions*
And in great foolishness
He shall go astray
And be lost.

REFORMERS

And she, being before instructed of her mother, said, Give me here John Baptist's head in a charger (*Matthew 14:8*).

Reformers
Are men who lose their heads
As John the Baptist.
He did no miracles
But spake only truth.
His raiment was camel's hair;
He ate *locusts and wild honey*.
His message was delivered
In a wilderness.

Kings felt his wrath;
Religious hypocrites felt the sting
Of his ridicule.
He was feared
Because he was just and holy.
A friend to the poor,
He sought to reform
A dying order,
Making an army of converts.
He refused their acclaim,
Insisting
That he must decrease
To make way for the increase
Of a new order.
This is a new day
Full of reformers
Who cannot reform.
Unwilling
To deny self,
To be holy and just,
Without humility,
Burning with misguided zeal.

THE FLOWER CHILDREN

A fool hath no delight in understanding, but that his heart may discover itself (Proverbs 18:2).

A fool is obsessed
With discovering himself—
He finds no pleasure
In the divine sentence of life.
The fool hath said in his heart
There is no God
And that life
Is a dry morsel—
A furnace
Fueled by wrath and violence.
So he shuts his eyes
And whispers to chief friends,
"Labor is in vain,
All is vanity
And vexation of spirit.
Come!
Let us eat the fruit of discovery;
Satisfy our bellies
With forbidden delicacies.
Let us discover

Our own hearts,"
He rages on,
Mocking life.
Of them it can be said,
Sluggards will not plow
When it gets cold.

WHERE IS WISDOM?

*But where shall wisdom be found? and where
is the place of understanding? Man knoweth
not the price thereof; neither is it found in the
land of the living (Job 28:12, 13).*

Wisdom,
Who can find it?
Where?
The depth saith, "It is not in me."
The sea saith, "It is not with me."
It cannot be gotten with *gold,*
Neither can *silver be weighed*
For the price thereof.

It cannot be valued ... precious onyx
Or ... sapphire.
It cannot be exchanged for jewels,
Not to mention coral or pearls,
For the price of wisdom
Is above rubies.
Whence then cometh wisdom?
Where is the place of understanding?
God understands
And He knoweth the place thereof.
He who *seeth under the whole heaven,*
Who measures the weight of wind,
Unto men He saith,
"Behold
The fear of the Lord—
That is wisdom.
To depart from evil—
That *is understanding.*
The fear of the Lord is the beginning
Of all wisdom.
He who would have wisdom,
Let him in love
Fear God
And forsake his sins."

THE THUNDER OF POWER

Lo, these are parts of his ways: but how little a portion is heard of him? but the thunder of his power who can understand (*Job 26:14*).

Man needs power
To help those without it,
To strengthen those without strength,
To counsel *him that hath no wisdom,*
To declare things as they really are,
To renew dead spirits,
To cover the naked destruction of hell.
God has all power
To stretch out the universe
Over empty places,
Hanging *the earth upon nothing.*
He binds up humidity in thick clouds,
Placing boundaries on the waters.
He divides *the sea with his power*
And he smites the proud.
By his spirit he garnishes *the heavens.*
He even created the crooked serpent,
But these are only glimpses of His power—
Only a little portion of Him that is heard.
He has promised power to all men.

After that the Holy Ghost
Has come upon them
And there will be thunder in that power—
Thunder against injustice,
Immorality and crime,
Thunder against hypocrisy
And the tyranny of small things,
Thunder against materialism
And hate.
But deeper still,
Love
Is the thunder of power.

CURSES ON COMMITTEES

Bring no more vain oblations; incense is an abomination unto me; the new moons and sabbaths, the calling of assemblies, I can not away with; it is iniquity, even the solemn meeting (Isaiah 1:13).

The ox knows *his owner,*
The ass his master's crib;
But my people do not understand
A wicked nation,
Burdened with evil—
Children that are corrupt,
Who have forsaken their God.
They have provoked the Holy One of Israel.
Revolution everywhere!
The whole head is sick
And the . . . heart faint.
From head to toe
There is no soundness;
But wounds,
Bruises,
Putrifying sores,
A country growing desolate,
Cities on fire.

What will the rulers in Sodom do
To relieve the oppressed?
Judge the fatherless?
Plead for the widow?
Judge unrighteousness?
They will call a solemn assembly—
A committee—
To offer a vain oblation
On phony altars of sacrifice.
And having fixed the blame,
Will go on to their appointed feasts,
The cause of the widow
Unresolved.

THE END OF ALL WARS

. . . and they shall beat their swords into plowshares, and their spears into pruninghooks: nation shall not lift up sword against nation, neither shall they learn war any more (Isaiah 2:4).

Enter into the rock;
Hide yourself *in the dust*
For fear of the Lord
And . . . the glory of His majesty,
For war shall be no more.
The lofty looks of man shall be humbled;
The haughtiness of men shall be bowed down.
He shall utterly abolish all idols.
They shall hide in caves
And cry for rocks to fall on them,
For God shall arise
To shake . . . the earth,
Casting down worshipers of silver and gold.
The man of war
Shall hide himself in the cleft of rocks.
He shall abide in darkness
Like the bat and the mole,
For the Judge of all nations shall rebuke him.

And it shall come to pass,
In the last days,
He will teach us His ways
And the law shall go out of Zion—
The word of the Lord from Jerusalem,
Swords to plowshares,
Spears to shears.
No nation shall lift a sword;
War shall be learned no more,
For the Prince of Peace
Shall be exalted
Above the hills.

THE MEASURE OF GOD!

Canst thou by searching find out God? canst thou find out the Almighty into perfection? It is as high as heaven; what canst thou do? deeper than hell; what canst thou know? The measure thereof is longer than the earth, and broader than the sea (Job 11:7, 8, 9).

Man would be vain.
Though he is *born like a wild ass's colt,*
His mouth is filled with talk
On the doctrine of God.
Where is He?
Let Him speak!
Make Him show us the secrets of wisdom,
The reason behind indignation and war,
Confusion and affliction—
Why He hunts for men like a fierce lion
While showing Himself marvelous to some.
Why did He bring us out of the womb?
To live so few days
In a land of darkness
Without order?
Living in the shadow of death
While life itself curdles like cheese

Only to go to dust again?
A multitude of words will never reveal
God!
He is past finding out,
Unsearchable,
Higher than heaven,
Deeper than hell.
What can man know about God?
He can only believe
His measure . . . is longer than earth,
Broader than the sea.

THE ETERNAL CITY IS COMING

*. . . the spirit . . . shewed me that great city,
the holy Jerusalem, descending out of heaven
from God. . . . her light was like unto a stone
most precious, . . . clear as crystal; . . . the
wall had twelve foundations . . . the city lieth
foursquare, and the length is as large as the
breadth . . . and the nations of them which
are saved shall walk in the light of it . . . the
gates of it shall not be shut . . . (Revelation 21).*

Science no longer scoffs
At God's eternal crystal city
Promised to future generations.
Consider the works of Paolo Soleri,
The Italian architect,
Who designed ecological cities:
The Hexahedron city,
A gleaming plexiglass structure,
Pyramiding 3500 feet into the sky,
Housing an entire city of 170,000 people;
Or the Babel Canyon
Twice as high as the Empire State Building,
A complete city tower for 250,000 dwellers;

And Arcuillage,
A transparent membrane
Hung from a cylindrical unit,
Housing a town of 30,000.
Science is beginning to confirm such a city
Can exist.
Man's secular city
Will harness modern technology
And build structures that stagger the mind of
     today,
But God's eternal city
Eclipses anything man can conceive.
For God's city
Will have no night,
No sickness,
No abominations,
No pollution;
And the Lamb of God
Will light the day.
Above all else,
The temple of God therein
Will contain
God's throne.

WHERE DOES IT ALL END?

Lord, make me to know mine end, and the measure of my days, what it is; that I may know how frail I am (Psalms 39:4).

Life is a vain show;
Men heap up riches,
Then die
Leaving it to others.
Man at his best state is vanity
And vexation.
His beauty consumes away like a moth.
He walks on earth as a stranger,
Waiting
For he knows not what.
Sorrow stirs his soul.
He holds his peace
Dumb with silence.
He muses in his heart
And a fire burns.
In his hand is the gift of life
But he muses on death,
Measuring his days,
Seeking to know
How it will end.

Then seeing it
Cries,
*"O spare me
That I may recover my strength
Before I go hence
And be no more."*
Life is a vain show.

GLORY, HONOR AND PEACE

*But glory, honour and peace, to every man
that worketh good, to the Jew first, and also to
the Gentile . . . (Romans 2:10).*

God has no favorites,
Rendering to every man
According to his deeds:
To them who despise his goodness
And longsuffering,
Wrath and judgment;
To those who judge others,
While doing the same things,

Hardness of heart,
Tribulation and anguish of soul;
To them who patiently continue in well doing,
Glory, honour and peace,
Immortality, eternal life.
Thou that judgest a man for adultery,
Dost thou commit adultery?
Art thou *an instructor of the foolish,*
A guide of the blind?
Dost thou teach thyself?
Therefore, blaspheme not the name of God.
Let your goodness
Exceed the goodness of Pharisees.
Make no provision for the flesh
To fulfill the lusts thereof,
And God shall give
Glory,
Honour,
Peace.

THE JUDGMENT OF GOD

*And enter not into judgment with thy serv-
ant: for in thy sight shall no man living be
justified (Psalms 143:2).*

I will never be good enough, God,
To be justified in Your presence.
My heart is inclined to evil,
To practice wicked works.
I eat the dainties
Of forbidden fruit.
Evil hunts me down
And I am held
By the cords of my own iniquity;
Therefore my spirit is overwhelmed
Within me.
I am left desolate,
Feeling unworthy,
Deserving only your judgment.
I stretch forth my hands to you.
Hear me speedily;
My spirit faileth;
I am headed for the pit.
Show me not judgment
And fear.

Cause me to hear Thy lovingkindness.
Let *me know the way*
Wherein I should walk.
Deliver me, O God.
I flee unto Thee
To hide me.
Justify my soul
Through the perfectness
Of Your own Son.

OUR FATHERS

*Our fathers have sinned, and are not; and we
have borne their iniquities* (*Lamentations*
5:7).

Our fathers have sinned
And are not,
And we pay for their iniquities.
Even the prophets and priests have failed,
Wandering as blind men
In the streets,

Polluting themselves among heathen.
The anger of the Lord hath divided them.
Our fathers gave over our inheritance
To strangers,
Our houses to aliens.
We are orphans and fatherless:
Our mothers are widows.
We are held in bondage.
Our necks are under persecution:
Servants have ruled over us.
We get our bread
By the peril of sword.
Our skin was black like an oven
From the heat of hate.
We are forced to pay
For what has always been ours.
Children come apart:
Young men are forced into the grind.
For this our heart is faint,
Our eyes are dim.
O Lord, . . .
Renew our days.

THE DISORDERLY

*Now we command you, brethren, in the name
of our Lord Jesus Christ, that ye withdraw
yourselves from every brother that walketh
disorderly, and not after the tradition which
he received of us (II Thessalonians 3:6).*

Paul prayed for the young
To *be delivered from unreasonable and wicked
   men*
Who had no faith,
But behaved themselves disorderly,
Trampling under foot the traditions of their
   fathers.
Paul said of the older generation,
They should be followed;
Their example was no delusion.
They labored in travail night and day,
Eating no man's bread for free,
Chargeable to no man
So they would be an example
Of diligence and free enterprise.
Their motto was clear,
If you don't work, you don't eat.
But now,

There are busybodies among you,
Working not at all,
But are loafers.
Withdraw yourselves from them,
For they are disorderly.
Have no company with them,
So they *may be ashamed.*
Count them not as enemies,
But admonish them as brothers,
For the Lord desires peace
By all means.

GOD IS FOR ME

I will cry unto God most high; unto God that performeth all things for me (Psalms 57:2).

I believe in a God who performs,
Who can *deliver my feet from falling*
And sustain me through every calamity.
When *I am afraid I will trust in* Him.
He will deliver my soul in peace

From the battle that is against me.
I will call on God
And He will save me.
He will bottle my tears
And mark my every step.
When I cry to Him,
My enemies will be turned back
Because *God is for me.*
In Him I put my trust.
I will not fear what man can do unto me;
My heart is fixed.
I will sing and give praise;
My soul shall be satisfied.
He will bring me through fire and flood
Into a desired haven.
He will cause his face to shine upon me
And daily load me with His benefits.
His face He will not hide,
But will hear me speedily.
He will never put me to confusion,
For He has give commandment to save me—
Because God is for me.

THE GOOD OLD DAYS

Say not thou, what is the cause that the former days were better than these? for thou dost not enquire wisely concerning this (Ecclesiastes 7:10).

Were the "nineties" really gay?
The "twenties" really innocent?
Were there any good old days?
Don't ask!
It is not wise,
For who knoweth what is good for man
In this life.
Speak not of gay times,
For *the heart of the wise is in the house of*
      mourning,
But the heart of fools is in the house of mirth.
Speak not of past years of song and dance,
For *it is better to hear the rebuke of the wise*
Than for a man to hear the song of fools.
Speak not of days of law and order,
For there is a time wherein one man ruleth over
      another
To his own hurt.
Speak not of days when work was honest,

For *all the labor of man is for his mouth,*
And yet his appetite is not satisfied.
This day is ours.
Wherefore I perceive that there is nothing better
Than that a man should rejoice in his own works,
For that is life's portion.
Who shall bring him to see
What shall be after him?
Our day will be envied
By those of tomorrow.

MAN IS DEAD

The man that wandereth out of the way of understanding shall remain in the congregation of the dead (Proverbs 21:16).

God is not dead.
Man is,
In his trespasses and sin,
Dead to God,
With his life having no purpose

Or meaning.
God is not sleeping:
Man is.
Sin entered the world
And death passed upon all men.
Those living in pleasure
Are dead while they live.
"These things saith he that hath the seven spirits
of God . . .
I know thy works,
That thou hast a name that thou livest,
And art dead."
"The man that wandereth out of the way
Of understanding
Shall remain in the congregation
Of the dead";
For the wages of sin is death.
To be carnally minded is death.
The soul that sinneth—it shall die.
The gift of God
Is eternal life.
Blessed are the dead
Who die in the Lord.
God lives—
Man dies.

DON'T MESS WITH CHRIST'S CHURCH

*Thy watchmen shall lift up the voice; with the
voice together shall they sing: for they shall
see eye to eye, when the Lord shall bring
again Zion (Isaiah 52:8).*

Christ's church is Zion
And the gates of hell shall not prevail against it.
She has not failed her generation.
God shall awaken her
To put on new strength
And shake off the dust.
Bands shall be loosed from her neck:
Her watchmen shall lift up the voice
Bringing good tidings to those of today.
A new song shall be heard.
They shall break forth in unity
And *see eye to eye,*
For the Lord shall stir Himself
And *bare His holy arm*
In the eyes of all nations.
The ends of the earth shall see . . .
Salvation and peace.
Let no man despise His church

Nor speak of her weakness,
For the church
Is Christ's bride.

STAY IN LOVE

*For I am persuaded, that neither death, nor
life, nor angels, nor principalities, nor powers,
nor things present, nor things to come, Nor
height, nor depth, nor any other creature,
shall be able to separate us from the love of
God, which is in Christ Jesus our Lord
(Romans 8:38, 39).*

Death is deep and dark.
Life is vanity and vexation of spirit.
Principalities and powers are immovable
Things present are uncertain:
Things to come unknown.
There are mysteries in the height and depth
Of this universe,
Yet none of these can *separate us*

From the love of God,
Which is in Christ the *Lord.*
Who shall separate us from His love?
Shall tribulation or distress?
Persecution or famine?
Nakedness, peril or sword?
No! For God is love.
This love *passeth all understanding*—
A bond of perfectness—
So walk in His love.
He that dwelleth in love
Dwelleth in God—
And God in him.

GOD HAS NO DARK SIDE

*This then is the message which we have heard
of him, and declare unto you, that God is
light, and in him is no darkness at all* (I John
1:5).

God is Light.
And if we walk in His *light,*
There can be no darkness,
And *we have fellowship* and love
One with another.
And here is how to know
If you walk in God's light.
Whoso keepeth His commandment,
In him is the love and light of God perfected.
And this is His commandment—
That you love your brother
Because the darkness is past
And the true light now shineth.
He that saith he walks in God's *light*
And hateth his brother
Is a liar
Who walks in darkness,
Knowing not where he goeth
Because of his blindness.

But let him that loveth,
Love not in word or tongue
But in deed and truth.
Hate is of the darkness
And God has no dark side.
If you would please Him,
Walk in His light
Which is love.

WHY DIDN'T SOME PREACHER TELL ME THAT BEFORE?

*Blessed are they whose iniquities are forgiven,
and whose sins are covered* (Romans 4:7).

The preacher cries, "Repent,
Humble yourself and admit you are a sinner,
Strip yourself of pride,
Hate your sins,
Confess them and all will be well."
So I obeyed,
Hoping for that blessedness

Of *sins covered* and *iniquities forgiven*,
But that was only the beginning of my battle.
The things I hate—I still do.
My foolishness overwhelms me
And I grieve the Holy Spirit again.
I admit I am weak, a poor sinner.
I know my sin is grievous;
I hate it—I want to change.
It has humbled me because it makes me weak.
I confess it constantly!
Where then is the power over it?
Then the word of the Lord came,
"Give up the struggle;
Quit trying to be good."
There is a rest, a place of peace,
Where by faith we get a true righteousness
Acceptable to God—
Christ's!
Yet if confessing and resting is the answer,
How can one enter into that rest?
Not by groping—
It, too, must be a gift from God.
Why didn't someone tell me before
To resign from the struggle
And ask God for the gift
Of rest?

JOSEPH—THE FIRST SOCIALIST

*And when all the land of Egypt was famished,
the people cried to Pharaoh for bread and
Pharaoh said unto all the Egyptians, Go unto
Joseph; what he saith to you, do (Genesis
41:55).*

Joseph,
The colorful visionary,
Was a righteous socialist
Who interpreted a prophetic dream
Of *seven years of famine*
In Egypt,
Following seven years of plenty.
Joseph is promoted to prime minister.
He harvests bumper crops,
Storing them in huge warehouses,
To sit out the famine.
The seven years of plenty ended
And the seven years of dearth began to come,
When all the land of Egypt was famished—
The people cried to the king *for bread.*
And Joseph opened the storehouses,
Selling corn to all who could buy
Until he had gathered all the money

To be found in Egypt,
And he brought it to the king.
When money failed
They cried again for bread,
And Joseph said,
"Give me your cattle
In exchange for corn."
And they brought their cattle,
Horses and flocks.
So *he fed them with bread* all that year,
While the government impounded the herd.
When that year was ended
They came . . . the second year,
Crying,
"Our money has failed
Our cattle are surrendered—
We have nothing left to offer
But our bodies
And our lands.
Buy us and our land
For bread and we . . . will be servants
To the government."
Better bled
Than dead.
And Joseph took over all the land of Egypt
For Pharaoh,

So the land became
Government owned.
As for the people,
They were removed from city to city,
And communes were established,
With one fifth of every harvest
Taxed to the government
Of Pharaoh.
The people thanked Joseph
And they said,
"Thou hast saved our lives;
We will be Pharaoh's servants."
Joseph, God's man,
Caused all Egypt
To sell out
For bread.
Yet Israel dwelt in Egypt, too,
But kept their possessions,
Growing and multiplying
Through private enterprise.
The lesson—
Socialism works only when administered
By righteous men.
Socialism works
For those who are satisfied
To be servants.

HELL AND HOPE FOR HOMOSEXUALS

. . . the men, leaving the natural use of the woman, burned in their lust one toward another; men working with men that which is unseemly, and receiving in themselves that recompense of their error which was meet (Romans 1:27).

The homosexual
Is already in hell—
His own—
Burning in his own lust,
Receiving in himself a recompense
For his error.
Loneliness,
A dishonored body,
Fear of never being delivered—
Condemned to a hell of desire
That cannot be quenched.
"But *thou are inexcusable, O man,
Whosoever thou art that judgest.*"
For when you judge them
In their hell,
"*Thou condemnest thyself*";
For thou doest deeds deserving wrath.

Would you judge them?
And knowing the goodness of God,
His *forbearance*
And longsuffering,
Would you deny them the same goodness
That led you to repentance?
God *will render to every man*
According to his deeds,
But He is no respecter of men.
He promises
Glory, honour
And peace
To every man,
To every homosexual,
Who fears God.
For all have sinned
And come short of the glory of God.
Blessed are they whose iniquities are forgiven
And whose sins are covered.
What shall we say, then,
To the homosexual
In his hell?
Believe on Him
Who justifies the ungodly
Through faith,
Offering free grace

Through redemption in Christ's name.
Stagger not at God's promise.
Be fully persuaded
That what He has promised
He is also able to perform—
Freedom from bondage.

THE REBEL WHO BLEW HIS CAUSE

For lo, thou shalt conceive, and bear a son;
and no razor shall come on his head: . . . and
he shall begin to deliver Israel . . . (Judges
13:5).

Samson, son of promise—
The rebel who blew his cause.
Born to a minority family,
Destined to overthrow the Establishment
Of his day,
He pursued his calling.
Ripping apart every beast
Who stood in his path,

He declared a one-man war
On the Philistine military-industrial complex—
A war-mongering hierarchy
Who kept his people in bondage;
Disposing their vineyards,
Enslaving the workers,
Preaching and practicing prejudice.
Samson became a political activist,
Burning, plundering
And looting.
This long-haired rebel shook the Establishment
So badly
The leaders cried for law and order.
His own downtrodden people,
Too weary and afraid to fight for freedom,
Turned him over
In chains
To the military.
But Samson still had a cause—
Civil rights for his people,
Equal justice for Hebrews.
The very thought aroused him.
Grabbing the *jawbone of an ass,*
He slew a thousand Philistine national guardsmen.
But then
On the very brink of success,

He is found in the grass
With harlots
And evil companions.
Tossing around riddles,
Pretending to be an intellectual,
He came apart—
Blew his cause.
The rebel is stripped of his power,
Mocked and scorned,
Blind and bald,
Destroyed and defanged
By permissive sex,
Excessive play and pleasure
And flirtation with forbidden evils.
In one final act of rebellion
He pulls down a house on his head,
And though three thousand died with him,
He is remembered
As the rebel who blew his cause.
Let every modern rebel open his ears to hear!
If your cause is so just,
If you are truly concerned,
What are you doing?
Sitting in the grass
Tossing around intellectual riddles?
Blowing pot?

Sleeping with little harlots?
Flirting with narcotics?
Beware!
You too will blow your cause,
Samson says.

COMMUNES

*Cast in thy lot among us; let us all have one
purse . . . (Proverbs 1:14).*

Let's all live together—
Share everything!
Come and join
The unhooked generation.
One roof—*one purse*—
Let us fill our house with love.
Beware, *my son,*
Hear the instruction of thy father:
Forsake not the law of thy mother.
If sinners entice thee,
If they say,

"Come with us,"
Walk not in their way.
Refrain your *foot from their path*
For their feet run to evil.
They do not hesitate
To lurk for the innocent,
Ensnaring them in a trap
Called freedom.
But it is a life of greed,
It is not a simple life—
Dropping out,
Doing your thing.
For these who all share one purse,
Who despise instructions,
Share only one thing—
The prosperity of fools.
They are deceived by their own devices.
Promising liberty,
They are bound.
Distress and anguish set in.
It is a path that inclineth to death.
It is a life of vanity—
The worst kind of pride—
Simple youth who have turned away.
And it shall destroy them
For the purse is a bag with holes in it.

O WRETCHED MAN

O wretched man that I am! who shall deliver me from the body of this death (Romans 7:24).

I am a wretched man—
There is a war in me.
The motions of sin rule my flesh.
A hunger for God consumes my spirit.
I want to *bring forth fruit* to God,
But sin dwelleth in me.
I know that in me there is *no good thing.*
For the good that I would [do],
I do not;
But the evil which I would not,
That I do.
What I hate,
That do I.
I have a will to do right,
To perform good;
But how to do it,
I find not.
I delight in God in the inward man,
But I am a captive
To my flesh—

I am a wretched man!
Who will deliver me?
It is like death.
I thank God,
Through Jesus Christ,
Condemnation—
Wretchedness—
Is crucified.

HALF-BAKED POLITICS

> *. . . Ephraim is a cake not turned. Strangers have devoured his strength, and he knoweth it not: yea, gray hairs are here and there upon him, yet he knoweth not (Hosea 7:8-9).*

America, land that I love!
Gray hairs appear here and there
Upon your head
And you know it not.
Strangers devour your strength
On battle fields everywhere,

Yet you knoweth not.
Pride testifies to our face.
We are *like a silly dove,*
Without heart.
They call here—they call there.
We go to the east, west and mid-east.
The net is spread upon them.
Our iniquity is discovered.
As troops of robbers we, too, have spoiled.
We have committed false crimes.
Our own doings have beset us about.
We have stretched out our hand to scorners.
We have slept while the fire consumed.
As a half-baked cake
We *have howled upon* our *beds* of ease.
Our arms have been strengthened.
We have assembled ourselves with corn and wine,
But we are a deceitful people
Who shall fall by the rage of deceitful tongues.
This shall be the *derision in the land*
That hath rejected its God
And moved on in its own mischief.

THIS LAND

Hear the word of the Lord, ye children of Israel: for the Lord hath a controversy with the inhabitants of the land, because there is no truth, nor mercy, nor knowledge of God in the land (Hosea 4:1).

God has a controversy with this land
Because truth is dying.
Mercy is wanting—
The knowledge of God is going.
There is swearing,
Killing, stealing and adultery everywhere.
They break out and blood toucheth blood.
The land is languished.
Fields are being destroyed—
The rivers and sea polluted.
People . . . strive with the priest—
The prophets fall in the night—
People are destroyed for lack of knowledge.
They are increased who sin grievously.
Hearts are set on iniquity—
They eat and have not enough—
They commit whoredom and are never satisfied:
Whoredom and wine have taken *away the heart.*

They burn incense and allow adultery—
Harlots are on every street.
The religious slide back,
As a backsliding heifer.
The revolters make a slaughter,
And the Lord withdrew Himself from the land
Till they acknowledge their offense
And seek His *face,*
And return to Him.

OLD GLORY IS GONE

As for Ephraim, their glory shall fly away like
a bird, from the birth, and from the womb,
and from the conception (*Hosea 9:11*)

Where has the old glory gone
From a nation that was the womb of freedom?
Are we now *a miscarrying womb?*
A land of *dry breasts?*
The prophets have become fools—

The spiritual man is mad!
Multitudes are in iniquity
And there is great hatred.
Hatred is in God's house
And prophets have become a snare.
The nation has deeply corrupted itself,
Being bereaved of its children
From its inception.
This land was planted in a pleasant place,
But now it is smitten—
The root is dried up.
We have become *an empty vine*
Bringing forth fruit only to ourselves.
Hearts are divided.
Altars have been broken down.
There is no respect for authority—
Judgment is perverted—
God's people are bent on backsliding.
The old glory is gone
Like a bird chased
From its place of birth.

EVEN HYPOCRITES HAVE THEIR MOMENTS

Knowest thou not this of old, since man was placed upon earth, That the triumphing of the wicked is short, and the joy of the hypocrite but for a moment? (Job 20:4, 5).

The hypocrite—
With his head reaching into the clouds,
Floating around in his dreams,
Chasing foolish visions in the night,
His bones are full of sin.
Wickedness is sweetness to his mouth.
He tries to hide it under his tongue.
The poison of asps churns within him.
He oppresses the poor,
Violently breaking up their houses.
Look at the wicked hypocrite
Wallowing in *brooks of honey and butter*—
Meat in his teeth—greed in his eyes.
He swallows down riches
And vomits up phony charity.
Knowest thou not since time began
His triumph is short?
His joy as a moment?

He shall not rejoice in his substance.
His belly shall not feel quietness.
Wrath *shall rain upon him*
Even while he eats.
Heaven shall reveal his iniquity
And the earth shall rise up against him.
This is *the heritage appointed . . . by God*
For hypocrites.

ANSWERS, GOD—THAT'S ALL I ASK!

Oh that I might have my request; and that
God would grant me the thing that I long for!
(Job 6:8)

I don't care if I come to the *grave in a full age*
Or do any great thing;
I request only peace and understanding.
Oh! *That God would grant me* this one *thing*—
Understanding for the things that touch my soul—
The poor who are devoured by the sword,
The innocent killed by the envy of foolish men

Who have taken root
And cursed our habitation,
Children who cannot live in safety
Crushed in the gates of our cities,
Born to trouble
Like sparks flying upward.
If I cannot understand,
And there is no peace,
Then let it . . . *please God to destroy me.*
Let Him *cut me off.*
I am so overwhelmed—
Hardened in my sorrow.
All around me, God, is terror.
Teach me
And I will hold my tongue.
Cause me to understand—
It is not in me to argue.
And there is no saint I wish to turn to.
You are the source.
Answers, God—that's all I ask!

UP AGAINST THE WALL

*He hath fenced up my way that I cannot pass,
and he hath set darkness in my paths (Job
19:8).*

Job was broken in pieces by the words of his
    friends.
Ten times they assaulted him, putting him down
While magnifying themselves.
But worse—
He thought God had overthrown him.
A net of confusion strangled his mind.
His cry for help fell to the ground.
Inside his soul,
He knew he was wrong,
But
Was he so wrong?
So evil
That he should be fenced in everywhere?
Every path blocked and black—
Hope gone—
Stripped of self-esteem
Like an enemy to God,
Friends and family running out?
STOP!
Job got to the source,

To the root of the matter,
With an iron pen.
Written in an eternal rock—
TRUTH—
The Redeemer still lives.
He will conquer the earth.
Worms may destroy this flesh,
But I will get to see God.
There will be a judgment—
I will not fear!

FALSE FACES IN THE DARK

The eye also of the adulterer waiteth for the
twilight, saying, No eye shall see me: and dis-
guiseth his face. The murderer rising with the
light killeth the poor and needy, and in the
night is as a thief (Job 24:15, 14).

The murderer is one who hates.
The adulterer one who steals.
Both are rebels against the Light.
They spend their time

Removing landmarks
And uprooting traditions.
Like *wild asses in a desert,*
They go forth looking for a prey.
They gather the vintage
Of wickedness.
They pluck the fatherless from the breast.
In the dark they dig through houses
Which they had marked for themselves in the
        daytime.
They walk only in the night,
And then only in disguise.
They destroy the poor and needy.
Thieves! Sinners!
I lay to their charge
Divorce and poverty,
Hate and fear.
As *drought and heat*
Consume . . . snow waters,
So will *the grave*
Devour these
Who move in the night
Behind a disguise.

TWO WAYS TO LIVE—ONE WAY TO DIE

One dieth in his full strength, being wholly at ease and quiet. His breasts are full of milk, and his bones are moistened with marrow. And another dieth in the bitterness of his soul, and never eateth with pleasure. They shall lie down alike in the dust, and the worms shall cover them (*Job 21:23-26*).

There was a wicked man
Who lived long and became mighty in power.
His offspring became established
In a house free from fear.
His cows calved—his bulls gendered.
His family spent *their days in wealth:*
None of them desired the knowledge of God.
He died in style,
Full of strength and in reputation.
His bones were moist with marrow
And worms covered him.
There was a righteous man
Who lived in bitterness of soul
And never ate with pleasure.
Driven like stubble before the wind,
As chaff carried by storms,

He drank from a cup of pain.
Hours were spent in isolation.
Nights of confusion
Forced him into a bed of tears.
He died in loneliness
And worms covered him.
In hell
The rich man called for water
To quench his parched tongue,
While poor Lazarus
Sat in Abraham's bosom.
It is hard *for a rich man to enter the Kingdom,*
So sell what you have above your needs
And give to the poor.

SHOW ME WHERE GOD SITS

Oh that I knew where I might find him! That I might come even to his seat! (*Job 23:3*).

I am troubled at God's presence.
The thought of Him makes my heart soft.
But I have a complaint—

I cannot seem to find Him
To approach His holy seat.
My mouth is filled with arguments
And I want to bring my cause to Him.
Will He turn on me with His great power?
No!
He would put His strength in me.
I esteem the words of His mouth
More than my necessary food.
I go forward
But He is not there—
Backward
But I cannot perceive Him.
I know He is at work
All around me,
But He seems to hide
That I cannot see Him.
I may never see the seat
Where God sits
Until judgment day.
But
He knows the way that I take.
When He has tried me,
I shall come forth as gold.
He will find me
Where I sit.

THE BREAD AND THE WINE

For they eat the bread of wickedness, and drink the wine of violence (*Proverbs 4:17*).

The bread of wickedness
And the wine of violence
Is the feast of fools
Who walk after the flesh
In the lust of uncleanness,
Despising government,
Self-willed,
They are not afraid to speak evil of dignitaries.
Rioting in the daytime
Against things they do not understand,
Sporting themselves with their own deceptions,
Their eyes are full of sex.
They cannot cease from their sins.
Beguiling, unstable souls—
Covetous—
They are wells without water,
Clouds carried about with every little tempest.
They speak swelling words of intellectual vanity,
Alluring the young
Through lusts of the flesh.
While they promise others liberty,

They themselves are the servants of corruption
Who bring others into bondage.
They who *eat the bread of wickedness*
And drink the wine of violence
Shall be cast down to hell,
Bound with chains of darkness.
Reserved to judgment
They shall be brought to swift destruction,
For they are false prophets
Preaching lies,
Making merchandise
Of those
Who know not the truth.
Ye shall know the truth
And the truth
Shall set *you free.*

WHERE WERE YOU WHEN GOD MADE THE WORLD?

Where wast thou when I laid the foundations of the earth? declare, if thou hast understanding (Job 38:4).

Finite mind,
Where were you
When God created this universe?
If you have such great understanding,
Tell me:
Where is the cornerstone of the universe?
Who shut the door to *the sea,*
That it should not break out over the land?
Where is the spring
That feeds the sea?
Have you *walked in the search of the depth?*
Have the gates of death been opened to you?
Where does light begin?
Who ignited the sun?
Hath the rain a father?
Who created drops of dew?
Can you change the course
Of a single star?
Can you send out lightnings

Or part the clouds?
Who sends *out the wild ass free?*
Who gave *goodly wings unto the peacock?*
Feathers unto the ostrich?
Hast thou given the horse strength
So that he mocks at fear?
Who gave the bird wisdom
To *stretch her wings to the south?*
Who made the eagle
Build *her nest on high* rock crags?
Shall the finite mind of man
Contend with the Almighty?
Will man instruct God?
Where was man
When God made the world?
Shall the clay
Argue with the potter?
Man is but a vapor,
The breath of God,
Locked in eternal lungs
Until God made him a habitation.

WHAT IS MAN?

*What is man, that thou art mindful of him?
and the son of man, that thou visitest him?*
(Psalms 8:4).

Man
Is *lower than the angels*
Yet crowned with a special glory
And honor.
For God gave him *dominion*
Over all *the works of* His *hands*—
All sheep and oxen
And beasts of the field,
The fowl of the air,
Fish of the sea.
The glory of man
Is not his intellect,
But the glory
Of a name—
God's name.
Set above the heavens,
Out of the mouth of babes
And suckling men,
God is glorified.
Consider the heavens—

The sun and moon,
The stars.
It is God's dominion.
The earth
Is man's dominion.
A man wrapped in God
Takes dominion
In His name.

THE SYSTEM IS ROTTING
AT THE FOUNDATION

If the foundations be destroyed, what can the
righteous do? (Psalms 11:3).

Help, Lord,
For the good man ceaseth.
The faithful fail
From among the children of men.
They speak vanity—
Everyone with his neighbor,
With double tongues

And *flattering lips.*
Men no longer live from the heart
But from the tongue.
The wicked walk on every side
And *the vilest men are exalted.*
They are all gone aside,
Filthy.
I want to flee like a bird
To my mountain,
For the foundations are being destroyed.
There is none that doeth good—
No, not one!
What can one person do
Who fears God?
Let him walk uprightly,
Working righteousness,
Speaking the truth in his heart.
Let him not backbite with his tongue,
Nor do evil to his neighbor.
Let him swear to his own hurt
And change not.
Let him give
Without reward.
He that doeth these things
Shall never be moved.

GOD MUST HATE ME

Thou art become cruel to me: with thy strong hand thou opposest thyself against me (*Job 30:2*).

Job said it—
I cry to God,
He does *not hear me*,
Terror has turned upon me.
My soul is poured out.
Affliction has *taken hold upon me.*
I have no rest in the night.
I am fallen into the dirt.
God makes me ride the wind.
Death haunts me
So I stretch out my hand
For His help.
I am being destroyed,
So I weep in my trouble.
When I looked for the good
And prayed for light,
Then evil came upon me—
There came darkness.
My bowels boiled.
I went mourning

Without the sun.
My flesh withers—
My bones burn—
Thou art become cruel to me.
Your *strong hand*
Opposes me
Doth not God *see my ways?*
Does He really *count . . . my steps?*
And number my hairs?
Let me be weighed
In an even balance,
And let God
See in me
Integrity.
He is my confidence.
I open all my doors
To His light.

JACOB—THE DELINQUENT

And he [Isaac] said, Thy brother came with subtilty, and hath taken away thy blessing. And he said, Is not he rightly named Jacob? for he hath supplanted me these two times: he took away my birthright; and, behold, now he hath taken away my blessing (Genesis 27:35, 36).

He was a delinquent,
By the measure of any generation,
Deceiving his blind father.
He stole his brother's inheritance
And Esau hated Jacob because of it.
Jacob fled his brother's wrath
And dwelt with his uncle Laban,
Where he fell in love with his daughter Rachel.
Laban said to Jacob,
"What shall be your wages?
You will not work for *me for naught.*"
Jacob said,
"*I will serve* you *seven years*
For Rachel, your *younger daughter.*"
After seven years,
Jacob said,

"Give me my wife."
So Laban made a great feast.
That night
Jacob entered the virgin's tent,
And only in the morning did he know
It was not Rachel
He had gone to,
But Leah, her older sister.
Laban deceived Jacob
To marry off his older daughter first.
Seven more years were spent
To purchase Rachel.
And those seven years were but as a day
Because of the love he had for her,
Even though married to Leah,
Her sister.
And Laban gave Rachel as wife to Jacob.
Jacob loved Rachel *more than Leah*,
Leah was hated
So God *opened her womb*,
Bearing Jacob six sons,
Hoping each time she conceived
He would be reconciled to her.
Rachel was envious
And forced Jacob to sleep with her maid
Who conceived a child,

Whom Rachel claimed as her own.
Leah then gave her maid to Jacob
Who also bore Jacob a son.
When Jacob came in from the fields at night,
Rachel and Leah hired him from one another
To visit their tents.
This man Jacob
Started his career on deception,
Lived in sexual turmoil,
Loving one wife
And despising the other,
Sleeping with maids.
Also interbred his own stock
With Laban's flock,
Leaving the weak and sick cattle behind.
Became a cattle baron
With thoroughbreds.
On deception,
Nevertheless,
The Scriptures declare
We serve the *God*
Of Abraham,
Of Isaac
And Jacob.
The God of Jacob?
Yes!

A God who saw beyond all his faults
To a heart so desperate
He wrestled with the angel of God
All night.
For he said,
"Unless God goes with me
I am a dead man."

A GOD FOR TIMES OF TROUBLE

Why standest thou afar off, O Lord? why hidest thou thyself in times of trouble? (Psalms 10:1).

I said in my heart
God has forgotten.
The poor are persecuted.
The wicked get their *heart's desire.*
Men are filled with hate;
They curse,
Deceive and defraud.
The innocent are murdered.

The favored few
Lurk in the villages,
Murdering the innocent
And depriving the poor.
Like *a lion in his den,*
They wait for the poor,
Drawing them into a net
Of helplessness.
You have seen it all, God—
The mischief and the spite.
Break the arm of the evil.
Hear *the desire of the humble.*
Judge the fatherless,
That men *of the earth*
May no longer oppress.
We are in trouble!
Come close.
If You seem to be hiding,
It is for the purpose
Of taking men
In their own devices.

HARLOTS—PROSTITUTES AND BAD SEX

For the lips of a strange woman drop as an honey comb, and her mouth is smoother than oil: But her end is bitter as wormwood, sharp as a twoedged sword. Her feet go down to death; her steps take hold on hell (Proverbs 5:3-4).

From *the window of my house*
I discerned a youth,
Void of understanding,
Walking into the harlot's trap.
In the twilight of *evening,*
In the black and dark of night
There met him a woman—
A subtle harlot.
She kissed him and said,
"My bed is perfumed and ready.
Come,
Let us take our fill of love."
With her much fair speech
She caused him to yield.
With the flattering of her lips
She forced him.
He goeth after her

As an ox goeth to . . . slaughter,
Until *a dart*
Strike through his liver,
Like a bird
Headed for a trap
Without knowing it.
Go not astray in her paths.
Many strong men have been slain by her:
Her house is the way to hell.
Going to her bed
Is a trip to the chambers of death.
Her disease is venereal.

WHO CAN UNDERSTAND HIS SINS?

Who can understand his errors? cleanse thou
me from secret faults (Psalms 19:12).

Will I ever understand
Why certain secret sins
Have dominion over me?
It is not hard

To acknowledge my sin.
Unto Thee
I confess my transgressions.
You will forgive them,
Yet the floods come again.
I fall.
I am held by the cords of my own iniquity.
My iniquities are gone over my head
As a heavy burden—
Too heavy for me.
I am troubled
By the disquietness of my heart.
My heart panteth for strength
While my foot slippeth.
I am sorry for my sin,
But it is stronger than I.
Innumerable evils have compassed me about.
I am not able to look up.
They are more than the hairs of my head.
Be pleased, O Lord,
To deliver me.
Cleanse me from secret sins.
I will no longer lean on my own understanding.
I resign—
Surrender.
Deliver me in your own way.

THE SHADOW OF SODOM

And the Lord said, Because the cry of Sodom and Gomorrah is great, and because their sin is very grievous, I will go down now, and see ... (Genesis 18:20).

Sodom—
A city without even ten good people,
Whose men, both old and young,
Went after strange flesh.
An affluent city—
Building, buying and selling
Until that day two angels appeared
As ambassadors of God
To warn Lot to evacuate
Before the fire should fall.
Was there a city so sinful
In all of history?
Hundreds of young and old men
Attempting the rape of two visiting angels—
Refusing the bodies of two virgin daughters—
So consumed by homosexual lust
They became violent beasts.
Lot escaped that city,
Leaving behind a wife

Petrified in a pillar of salt.
Lot and his two daughters
Dwelt in a cave,
In the mountains of Zoar.
And while Sodom still smoldered
The two daughters
Made their father drunk,
Laid with him,
Committing incest and
Getting even with a father
Who had offered them to a sex-crazed mob in
    Sodom.
The fire and brimstone did not succeed
In burning out sin.
Which is worse—
Sodomy or incest?
Is it any wonder God sent His Son
As an ultimate solution
To the sin problem!
Water and blood could not drown it
And fire could not burn it,
But Calvary covered it.
The shadow of Sodom
Is superimposed
By the shadow
Of a cross.

NEW EVERY MORNING

*It is of the Lord's mercies that we are not con-
sumed, because his compassions fail not. They
are new every morning (Lamentations 3:22-23).*

We would all be consumed
Because of our wickedness,
Had it not been for God's mercies.
They are fresh and *new every morning.*
God *is merciful and gracious,*
Slow to anger,
And of great kindness.
Soft in heart to those who repent,
He retaineth not His anger . . .
Because He delighteth in mercy,
Pardoning iniquity.
He delights not in the death of the wicked,
But offers universal mercy
To every transgressor;
But let him who receives mercy
Be merciful.
Blessed are the merciful:
For they shall obtain mercy.

THE CRUCIFIED MILITANT

He was oppressed, and he was afflicted, yet he opened not his mouth: he is brought as a lamb to the slaughter, and as a sheep before her shearers is dumb, so he openeth not his mouth (Isaiah 53:7).

Christ was a true militant—
Fighting for other men's rights,
Driving money changers from God's church
And letting the oppressed go free;
Yet he himself *was oppressed . . .*
And afflicted,
Misunderstood and rejected.
His own rights were denied Him:
A jury perjured Him.
Priests aroused the silent majority
With lies and half truths.
He was brought as a lamb to the slaughter.
They plucked His beard
And spit on His face.
The highest court in the land
Was prejudiced against Him;
Yet this mighty militant
Opened not his mouth

And in his sorrow claimed no rights.
He poured out His life
As *an offering*
To justify the rights of all men.

ROLLING STONES GET NO SATISFACTION

Wherefore do ye spend money for that which is not bread? and your labour for that which satisfieth not? harken diligently unto me, and eat ye that which is good, and let your soul delight itself in fatness (Isaiah 55:2).

Thousands gather at music festivals—
Rolling stones looking for satisfaction,
Hungering and thirsting,
Working hard at finding peace,
Drinking at every cistern of new experience,
Eating forbidden fruit.
Their flowers are pierced with thorns
And love is soured by greed.

There is no satisfaction on earth
And all labor is in vain;
Yet to those who will listen diligently,
There is a promise from God
Of TRUE satisfaction.
To those who seek the Lord
And forsake wicked ways—
Abundant pardon,
Rain upon dry ground,
Fatness for the soul,
Goodness and fullness to the eater
And a going forth in peace.
He asks only that we stand still
To see His salvation.
Jesus satisfies.

BLACK IS BEAUTIFUL

*I am black, but comely. . . . Look not upon
me, because I am black, because the sun hath
looked upon me . . . they made me the keeper
of the vineyards; but mine own vineyard have
I not kept* (*Song of Solomon* 1:5-6).

She was King Solomon's lover—
A type of the church of Christ,
And she was black—
Beautifully black,
As black *as the curtains of Solomon.*
She was despised on every side,
So busy keeping others' vineyards
Her own were neglected;
But a new day came
And she was exalted above all others,
A . . . *lily among thorns.*
She entered the king's banqueting hall
And the banner over her was love.
No longer a servant,
This beautifully black maiden
Ravished the heart of a king,
Who told her—
"Thou art all *fair, my love;*

There is no spot in thee."
He saw beyond her skin,
And as God does,
He looked on her heart.

THE POVERTY BAG

*I know both how to be abased and I know
how to abound: everywhere and in all things
I am instructed both to be full and to be hun-
gry, both to abound and to suffer need
(Philippians 4:12).*

This generation has not learned how
To live with affluency.
Sons and daughters of the wealthy
Run from their riches and wealth,
Living as homeless waifs,
Choosing poverty as their bag.
Paul, the Jewish rebel, experienced both poverty
and wealth,
Learning how to suffer need

And how to abound in fullness.
He said,
"I have learned in whatsoever state I am,
Therewith to be content."
Forsake not your wealth and name
In the guise of self-sacrifice and humility.
It is phoniness,
Proving only that you cannot face the responsi-
    bility
Of using what you have
To help those who are honestly poor.
God save us all
From the poor rich kind,
Seeking their own salvation
By running from Father's house.
Return—sell what you have
And give to the poor.

WHICH WITCH?

*Now the works of the flesh are manifest,
which are these. . . . Idolatry, witchcraft . . .
I tell you . . . they which do such things shall
not inherit the kingdom of God (Galatians
5:19-21).*

Which witch will be most famous tomorrow?
Which soothsaying prophet will rise to new prom-
    inence?
Will astrology, black magic—
Satanism, spiritualism, or occultism
Find the most converts?
The masses now flock to these fortune tellers.
Their books flood the world
And mankind is ready
For their kind,
Because this is a generation of idolators,
Walking in the flesh
And the works of the flesh,
Include witchcraft and false prophesying.
I tell you,
Flee from them all;
For *they which do such things*
Shall not inherit the kingdom of God.

The occult is a poisoned cistern,
And those who drink its waters
Will be clothed with death.

THE PRICE OF UNBELIEF

*Then Jesus answered and said, O faithless and
perverse generation, how long shall I be with
you? how long shall I suffer you (Matthew 17:17)?*

Unbelief is man's number one sin.
It is a defiant act of self-will
That leads to perverseness of the flesh.
Where there is unbelief and cynicism
There is also perverseness of every kind.
Show me a man who boasts God is dead
And that Christ was not divine,
That faith is foolishness,
And I will show you a man
Who becomes a God to himself,
Indulging without conscience

And experimenting with acts of moral depravity.
This has become a generation of unbelief,
And that is why it is a generation
Completely immoral,
Lusting after the very perversions
That destroyed Sodom and Rome.
God will not put up with it long,
And man's unbelief and doubt
Has never in history
Stopped fire and brimstone from falling.

LIBERTY IS NOT A LICENSE!

*For, brethren, ye have been called unto liberty;
only use not liberty for an occasion to the flesh,
but by love serve one another (Galatians 5:13).*

The rebel cries liberty
For the oppressed black,
The neglected Indian tribes,
Mexican wetbacks and West Coast grape pickers.
They call for liberty on campus—

For colonies and emerging nations.
They behave as though liberty
Were their discovery and brainchild,
But God says
Man is *called unto liberty*—
Divinely destined and called.
Only liberty must not be used as a license
To appease the flesh,
To indulge in wreckless pleasure and sensuality—
As a badge of liberty.
But man is called to liberty
Only to free himself for service to others,
By love, serving one another
Peaceably and nonviolently;
For if the rebels continue to bite and devour
In the guise of liberty,
They will only consume one another.

THE CURSING COAT

As he loved cursing, so let it come unto him: as he delighted not in blessing, so let it be far from him . . . he clothed himself with cursing . . . (Psalms 109:17-18).

Cursing is the fashion of modern rebels—
A coat worn by revolutionaries
To shock the Establishment.
They curse society,
Religion,
Judeo-Christian values,
Puritan morals,
Parental discipline
And nearly all government agencies.
They wear rhetoric and threats
Like sports coats.
It seems to fit their style of revolution.
But those who clothe themselves with cursing
Like a garment—
It shall *come into* their own *bowels like water*
And like oil into their *bones.*
Like a restricting girdle
It shall bind them.

One revolutionary act of love
Accomplished more than all the cursing
Of an army of rebels.